For Bix, Babeface, Mi and Er

Published by The Baben
Evanston, IL

All rights reserved.
No portion of this book may be reproduced in any form without permission from the publisher, except as permitted by U.S. copyright law.

ISBN 978-0-578-31827-1

Copyright ©2021 The Baben

This book is a work of fiction. Names, characters, events, and incidents are the products of the author's imagination. Any resemblance to actual persons, living or dead, or actual events is purely coincidental.

www.booksbythebaben.com

3 5 7 9 10 8 6 4

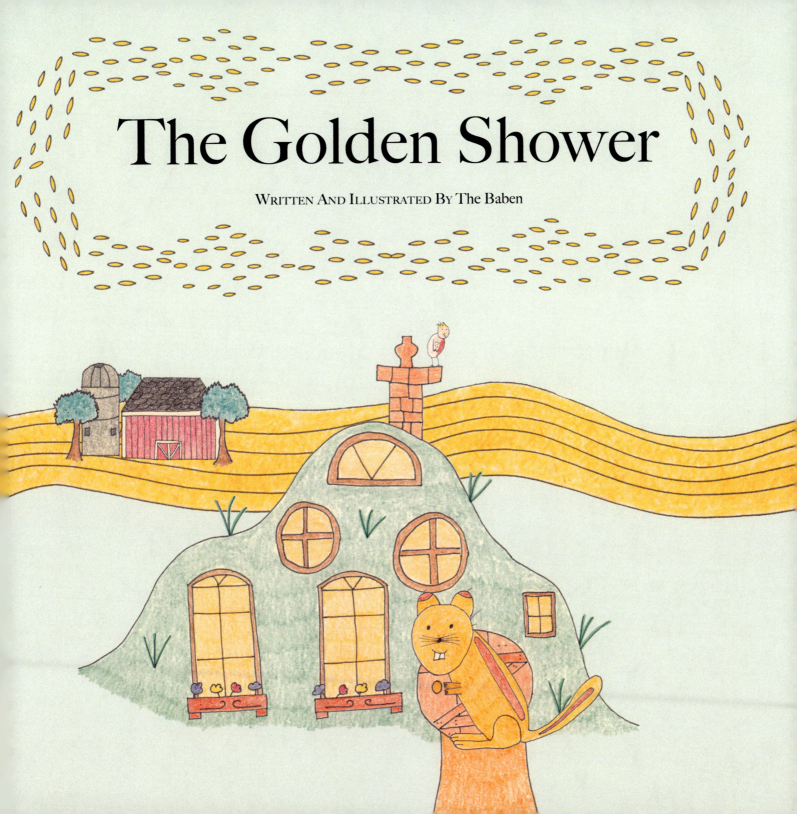

Winston the chipmunk lived in a cozy burrow among soaring maple trees.

His home was just beyond a sea of rolling wheat fields.

He led a rather normal, and slightly boring,
life for a chipmunk.

Every morning he rose before sunrise to
sweep his front stoop and wash his whiskers.

Winston's favorite part of the day was
foraging for his favorite meal:
blueberries, wheat kernels, and chestnuts.

Unfortunately, only blueberries were easy
to find in the meadow.

Grains and nuts were a special treat.

Sometimes, Winston thought about looking
for grains and nuts elsewhere, but he didn't
like to stray too far from home.

He knew his meadow well, and besides,
he didn't want to risk getting lost.

However, now and again Winston ventured to
the neighboring meadow to visit
his best friend Franklin.

It was a curious friendship because Franklin was different from Winston in nearly every way.

Instead of rising early, Franklin liked to stay out late and sleep in.

Instead of following a schedule, Franklin's days were filled with spontaneous adventures.

Instead of staying close to home, Franklin often traveled to the distant farm beyond the meadow to pilfer wheat and chestnuts.

Despite these differences, Winston and Franklin
had a close friendship.

Franklin was a good storyteller and Winston's favorite
pastime was listening to Franklin's daring
exploits at the farm.

Winston would often stay up past
his bedtime listening to Franklin's stories.

"You really fit your entire fist in there?"
Winston asked in disbelief as Franklin regaled
him with another one of his adventures from the farm.

"I sure did!
It wasn't easy, but I got my hand in."
Franklin replied.

"I pulled out a fistful of wheat, but the
hole in the barn was so small that my hand nearly
got stuck the second time," he laughed.

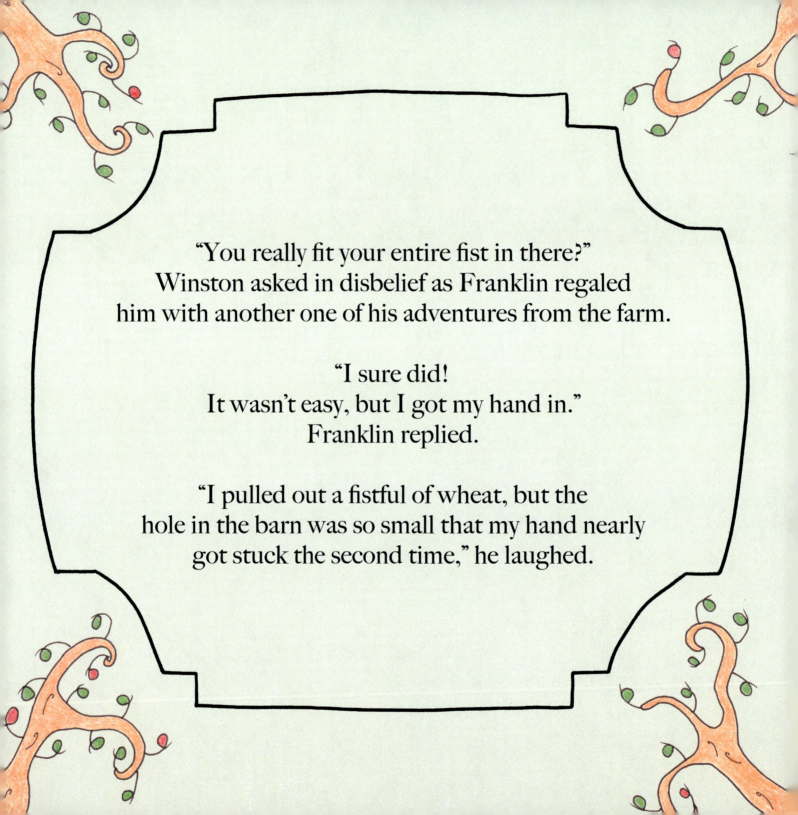

So it went, with Franklin feasting on wheat
and chestnuts while Winston stuck to
his bland diet of berries.

Although he would never admit it to Franklin, Winston
often fantasized about traveling to the farm beyond
the meadow to star in his own adventure.

Little did he know, that day was just around the corner.

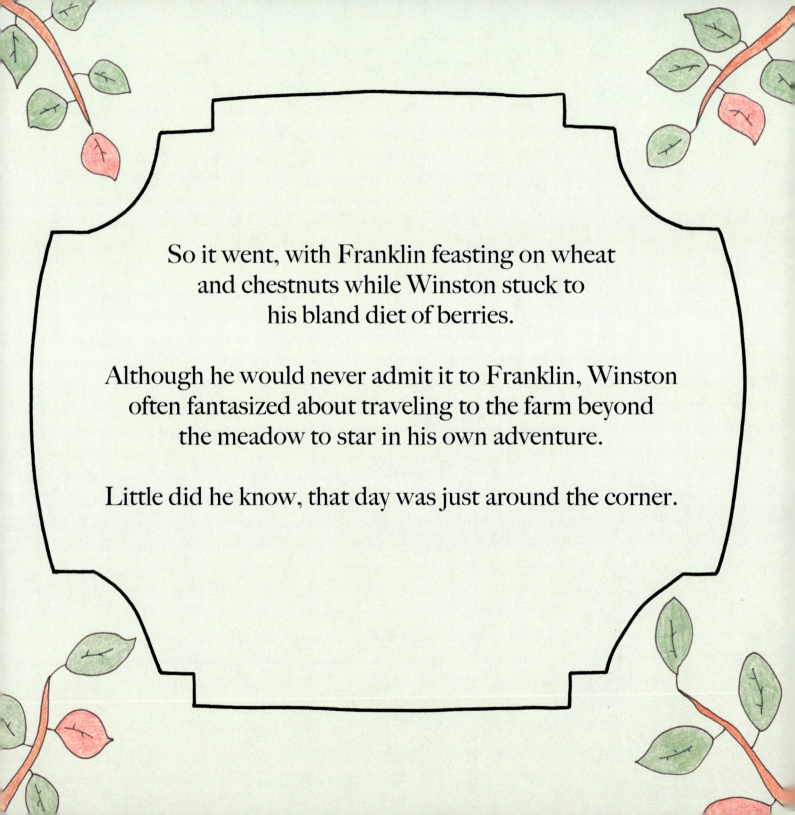

One afternoon Winston walked over to Franklin's house as he usually did when the weather was particularly pleasant.

As he approached he saw Franklin standing in front of his burrow, and he could tell that something was different.

"Winston!" Franklin yelled,
"Isn't your birthday next Saturday?"

"Well…yes," Winston answered hesitantly.

"Perfect!" Franklin replied.
"Something happened to me at the farm last night,
and I haven't been the same since."

"It was so unexpectedly wonderful that I
arranged the same thing for you,
as a birthday present!"
he exclaimed.

"What is it?" Winston asked as he sat down.

"It's a surprise," Franklin said with a grin, "but at the farm, they call it a golden shower."

"I've never heard of that," said Winston.

Winston was reluctant to visit the farm,
but he had never seen Franklin
so excited before.

"I don't know about this..." Winston said.
"How do I even get a golden shower?"

"You need to find a chipmunk named Candy.
She lives near the base of the silo, but she is
only there on weekends," Franklin explained.

"Candy? That's a strange name," Winston remarked.

"When you find her, tell her I sent you.
She will know what to do,"
Franklin said.

The day had come and it was finally
Winston's birthday.

He spent the previous week trying to figure out
what was in store for him at the farm, but he could
not guess what a golden shower might be.

He did discover one detail though—
Franklin had told him that golden showers were
not free. Since it was a birthday present, Franklin
helped Winston gather berries to trade.

I hope I don't regret this Winston thought
to himself as he started off
toward the farm.

By mid-day, Winston was approaching the silo next to the barn.

He stopped on a small hill overlooking the silo and waited for any sign of movement.

There! A slender silhouette emerged from behind a chestnut tree near the silo.

It had to be Candy.

Winston scurried up and asked hesitantly,
"Are...are you Candy?"

"Hi there," she said sweetly.
"Yes, I am Candy. What can I do for you?"

"Franklin sent me, he said that you would know
what to do. He talked about a golden shower,"
Winston said sheepishly as he held
out the berries he had brought.

"Ahh yes, one of my specialties,"
Candy replied.

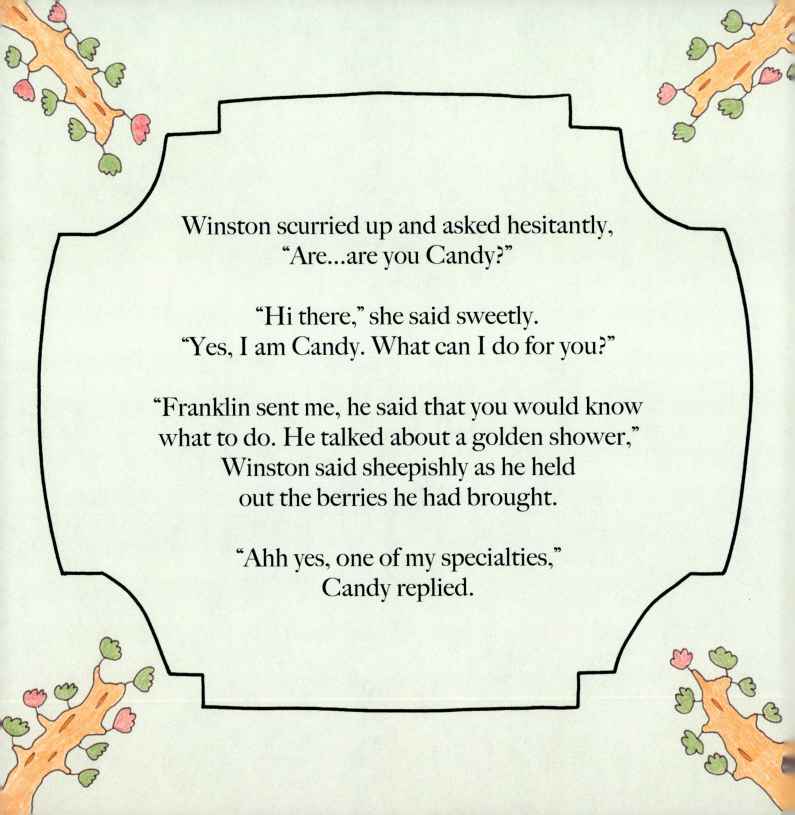

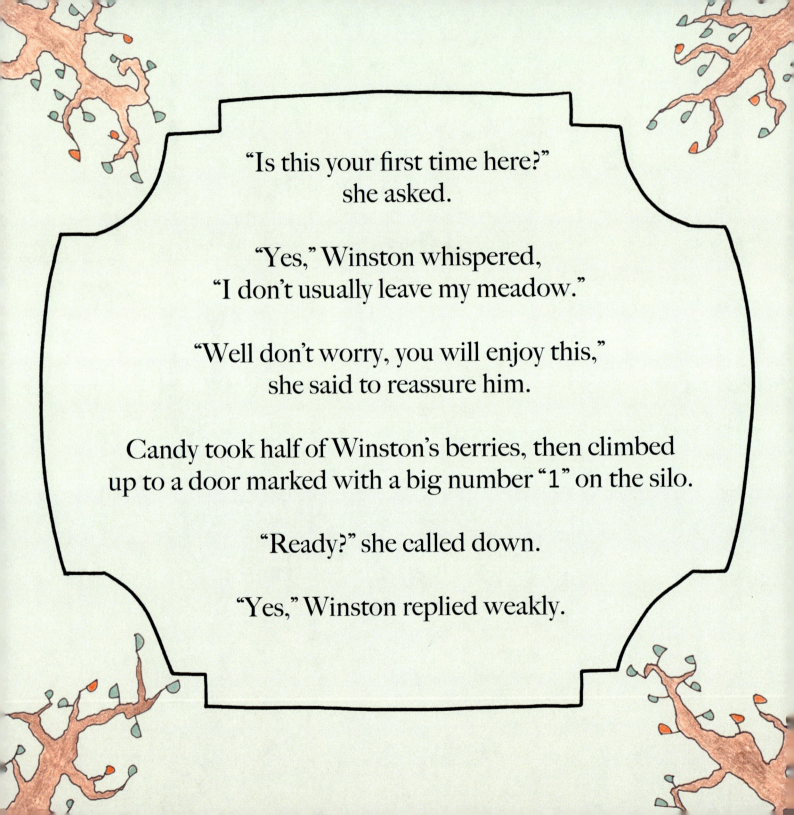

"Is this your first time here?"
she asked.

"Yes," Winston whispered,
"I don't usually leave my meadow."

"Well don't worry, you will enjoy this,"
she said to reassure him.

Candy took half of Winston's berries, then climbed
up to a door marked with a big number "1" on the silo.

"Ready?" she called down.

"Yes," Winston replied weakly.

Candy pried open the door and golden
kernels of wheat came pouring down on Winston.

I should have known! he thought to himself.
What a treat!

He was so happy he could hardly breathe.
He rarely ever got to eat wheat, and never so much
all at once. He was having such a good time that
he barely noticed Candy had shut the door.

"That's all I can do for today,"
Candy yelled down.
"Do you want some time to clean up?
I can get you a towel if you'd like."

"No thanks, I'm just fine!"
Winston exclaimed.
He picked a few stray grains from his
whiskers and popped them in his mouth.

As Candy descended, Winston's eyes
strayed to the back door of the silo.

It had a big number "2" on it.

"What about the back door?" Winston asked.
"You know, number 2?"

Candy hesitated.
"That is…a bit more difficult," she said.
"I've tried before, but nothing came out.
It takes a lot of work, and some luck."

"However," she continued,
"I could give it a try for the rest of your berries."

"Ok!" Winston said as his curiosity rose.

Candy climbed up to the second door and squatted down to get into a good position.

"Are you ready?" she shouted down to Winston.

"Yes!" Winston said confidently.

Candy strained with all her might and the back door burst open.

This time, something came out.

It was magical.

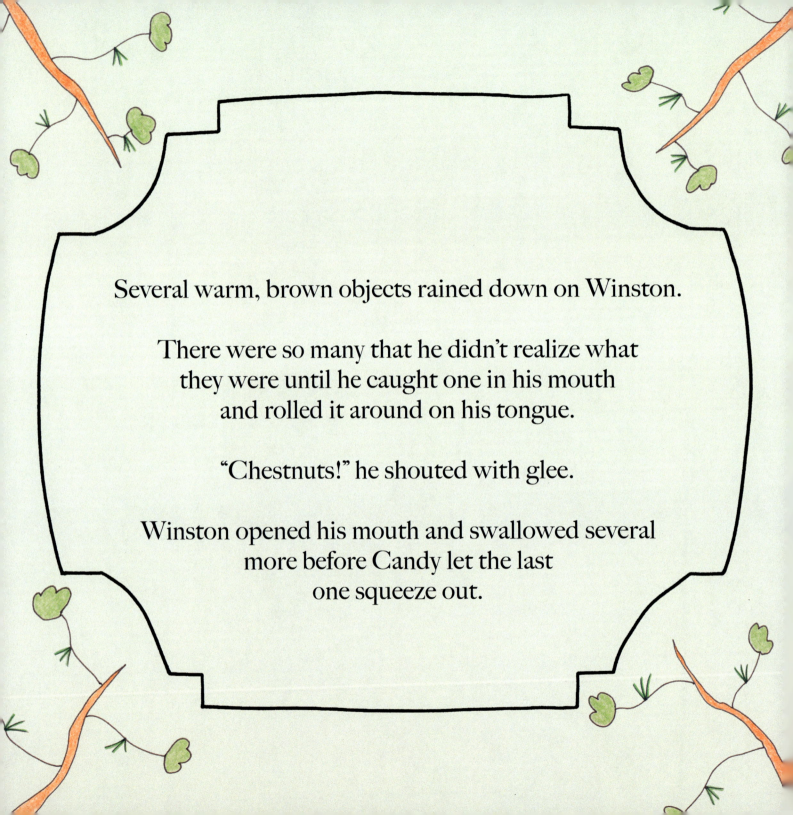

Several warm, brown objects rained down on Winston.

There were so many that he didn't realize what they were until he caught one in his mouth and rolled it around on his tongue.

"Chestnuts!" he shouted with glee.

Winston opened his mouth and swallowed several more before Candy let the last one squeeze out.

When Candy climbed back down to
the ground Winston said,
"That was an amazing experience.
Thank you so much!"

Candy laughed.
"I'm here most weekends, so you can always
come back," she said.

"I will!" Winston said over his shoulder
as he started home.

I can't wait to tell Franklin,
he thought to himself.

As he arrived at Franklin's house he barely got to the door when Franklin threw it open and exclaimed, "How was it?"

"I had that golden shower you talked about, and I liked it a lot!" Winston beamed.

"I told you!" Franklin cheered.

Franklin leaned in and wrinkled his nose. "What is that smell?" he asked.

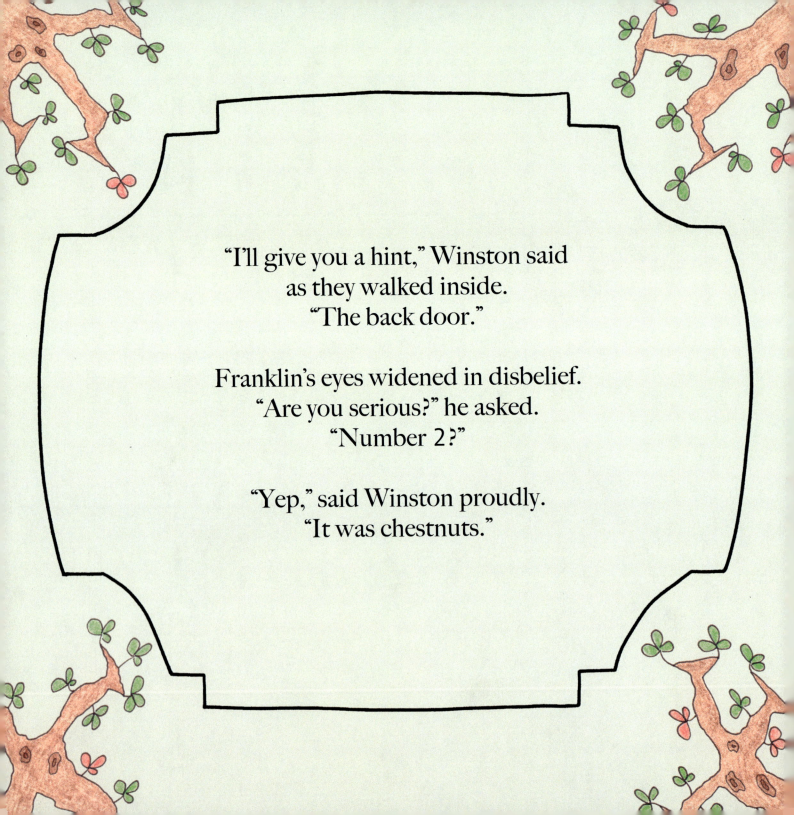

"I'll give you a hint," Winston said
as they walked inside.
"The back door."

Franklin's eyes widened in disbelief.
"Are you serious?" he asked.
"Number 2?"

"Yep," said Winston proudly.
"It was chestnuts."

Franklin was very impressed.

"I never thought I'd see the day when you tried something before me!" Franklin said.

"I think Candy likes me," said Wiston. "She said I can come back any weekend."

Franklin chuckled and said, "I think she says that to everyone, Winston."

"Even so," Winston said, "I had a great time."

For once, it was Winston who regaled Franklin with stories late into the night.

If you like this book please support us with an Amazon review!

Visit www.booksbythebaben.com to join our mailing list and be the first to hear about new titles.

Adulting (inspired by stuff grown-ups do)

Get a plant, they said.
It'll be fun, they said.

Meet Gobb Pucking Bammit,
Pizza Bucking Bit, Howlee Sitt,
and other silly potty mouth
monsters in this soon-to-be-
award-winning children's book.

Things That Go (no explanation needed)

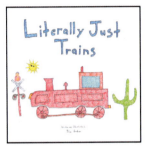

The title says it all.
If your kid loves trains then they
will love this book.

The title says it all.
If your kid loves garbage trucks
then they will love this book.

Pen Fifteen Club (innocent stories full of innuendo)

Henry has a paintbrush, but no paint.
Cindy has paint, but no paintbrush.
When they discover their
complementary interests Henry and
Cindy work together to make their
dreams come true.

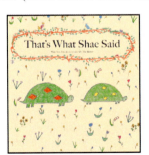

The journey will be long and hard.
That's what Shae said!
Join Shelly and Chester as they follow
advice from the wise owl Shae and
search for a new pond to call home.

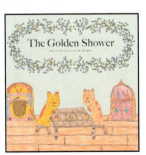

Relax, they're just chipmunks,
and it's a golden shower of *wheat*.
Get your mind out of the gutter.